Franklin Watts
96 Leonard Street
London EC2A 4RH

Franklin Watts Australia
14 Mars Road
Lane Cove
NSW 2066

ISBN: UK Edition 0 7496 0162 0

A CIP catalogue record for this book
is available from the British Library.

© Franklin Watts 1990

Editor: Kate Petty
Design: K & Co

Typeset in England
by Lineage, Watford
Printed in Italy by
G. Canale S.p.A., Turin

Ways to....

BUILD *it!*

Henry Pluckrose

Photography by Chris Fairclough

FRANKLIN WATTS

London • New York • Sydney • Toronto

Lots of different materials are used for building.

Many things are built in brick. Bricks are made from clay and baked to make them hard.

Bricks are joined together with mortar. Mortar is a mixture of sand, cement and water.

Stone is also used for building. It can be sawn into building blocks and shaped with a chisel.

Glass is also a building material. It is usually clear so that it lets the light come through.

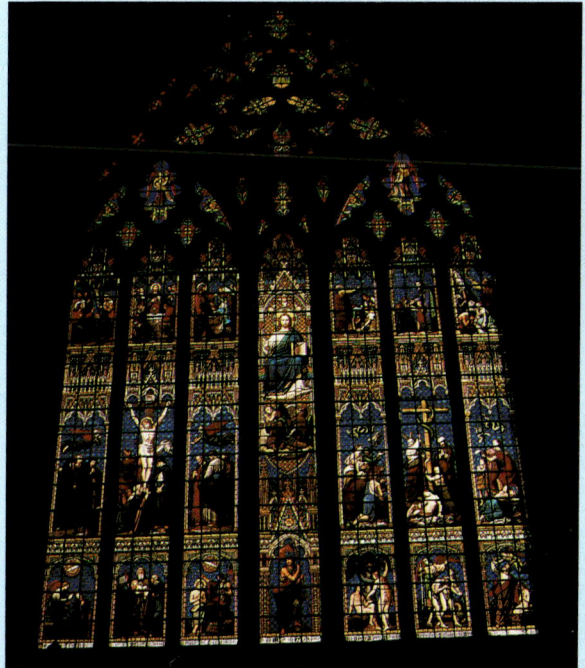

Some things are
built in wood.
What else is
needed for building
with wood?

Wood is often painted or stained or varnished to protect it.

Houses can be built from bricks, stone, glass and wood. What else might be needed ...

... tiles for the roof, pipes for water and special cables to bring in electricity?

A completed building still needs some finishing touches. Where might you find these?

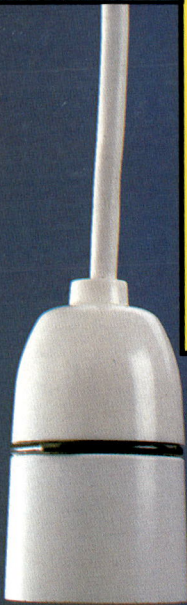

shavers only

200 – 250 v. a c

Buildings give
protection from
wind and rain,
sun and snow.
They have to be
strong ...

... but even the strongest building may be damaged by storms, floods or earthquakes.

Homes are built in different ways all over the world.

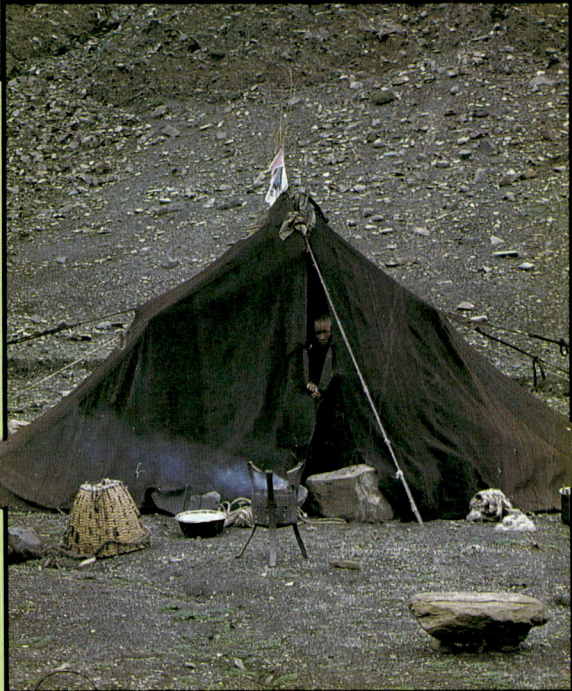

Sometimes people make homes from the materials that are easiest to get hold of.

We need buildings for many purposes. Can you match these pictures?

What are these different buildings called? Does anybody live in them?

Things to do

● You can build your own house, palace, castle or town in the sand. First collect some different shaped containers (yoghurt pots, small boxes, toy bucket). Make the sand damp. Pack the containers with damp sand and use them as moulds to make your building.

● Use wooden bricks to build a tower. Can you build a tower 8 bricks high? What is the highest tower you can build? Now try to build a tower on a sloping surface. What happens when you try to build high?

● Look at the patterns which bricks make in a wall. Try to find different patterns: some like this

some like this

How many more kinds of pattern can you find?

● Find some wooden bricks like these.

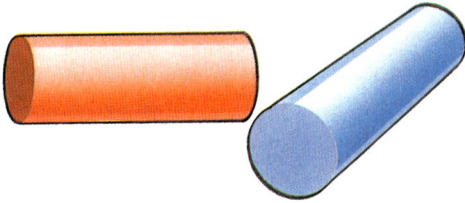

Use them to hold a roof like this.

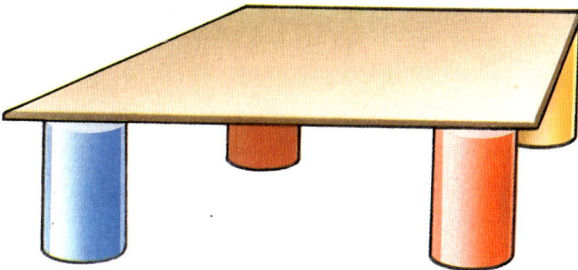

Can you use bricks like these to build a wall?

● How many different kinds of things (wood, brick, stone, metal, plastic) have been used to build your school? How many can you find
— on the inside?
— on the outside?

Words about building

	Building materials
add	brick
assemble	cement
builder	cobble
built over	concrete
built up	earth
carve	iron
colour	mortar
construct	plank
cover	plastic
cut	sand
decorate	slate
erect	steel
heap	stone
join	switch
make	tile
mass	timber
paint	thatch
pile	wire
produce	wood
put together	
raise	
shape	
tool